CHARTED DECORATIVE INITIALS

A Complete Alphabet Embellished with Birds and Flowers

Misse Moeller

DOVER PUBLICATIONS, INC.
NEW YORK

Copyright © 1984 by Misse Moeller.
All rights reserved under Pan American and International Copyright Conventions.

Published in Canada by General Publishing Company, Ltd., 30 Lesmill Road, Don Mills, Toronto, Ontario.
Published in the United Kingdom by Constable and Company, Ltd.

Book Design by David K. Andersen

Charted Decorative Initials: A Complete Alphabet Embellished with Birds and Flowers is a new work, first published by Dover Publications, Inc., in 1984.

Manufactured in the United States of America
Dover Publications, Inc., 31 East 2nd Street, Mineola, N.Y. 11501

Library of Congress Cataloging in Publication Data

Moeller, Misse.

Charted decorative initials.

(Dover needlework series)
1. Cross-stitch—Patterns. 2. Initials. 3. Decoration and ornament—Animal forms. 4. Decoration and ornament—Plant forms. I. Title. II. Series.
TT778.C76M64 1984   746.44   83-20551
ISBN 0-486-24646-9

Introduction

Decorative initials are widely sought by needleworkers who wish to add a distinctive touch to pillows, wall hangings, samplers, tote bags, clothing and many other projects. This excellent collection contains a complete alphabet of initials embellished with birds and flowers. The 26 letters embody the elegance, simplicity and originality for which Scandinavian designs are renowned. To give inspiration, all of the designs are shown in full color on the covers of this book.

The designs are charted for ready use in different forms of needlework such as counted cross-stitch, needlepoint, latch-hooking, crochet and knitting. Keep in mind that the finished piece of needlework will not be the same size as the charted design unless you happen to be working on fabric (or canvas) that has the same number of threads per inch as the chart has squares per inch. With knitting and crocheting, the size will vary according to the number of stitches per inch.

To determine how large a finished counted cross-stitch design will be, divide the number of stitches in the design by the thread-count of the fabric. For example, if a design that is 112 stitches wide by 140 stitches deep is worked on a 14-count cloth, divide 112 stitches by 14 to get 8 and 140 by 14 to get 10; so the worked design will measure 8″ x 10″. The same design worked on 22-count fabric would measure approximately 5″ x 6½″.

Most of these designs were originally created for counted cross-stitch; one of the great advantages to this craft is that the supplies and equipment required are minimal and inexpensive. You will need:

1. A small blunt tapestry needle, #24 or #26.
2. Evenweave fabric. This can be linen, cotton, wool or a blend that includes miracle fibers. The three most popular fabrics are:

Cotton Aida. This is made 14 threads per inch, 11 threads per inch, 8 threads per inch, and so forth. Fourteen, being the prettiest, is preferred.

Evenweave Linen. This also comes in a variety of threads per inch. Working on evenweave linen involves a slightly different technique, which is explained on page 5. Thirty-count linen will give a stitch approximately the same size as 14-count aida.

Hardanger Cloth. This has 22 threads per inch and is available in cotton or linen.

3. Embroidery thread. This can be six-strand mercerized cotton floss (DMC, Coats and Clark, Lily, Anchor, etc.), crewel wool, Danish Flower Thread, silken and metal threads or pearl cotton. DMC embroidery thread has been used to color-code all of the patterns in this book. One skein of each color given in the color key is needed, unless otherwise indicated in parentheses. For 14-count aida and 30-count linen, divide six-strand cotton floss and work with only two strands. For more texture, use more thread; for a flatter look, use less thread. Crewel wool is pretty on an evenweave wool fabric, and some embroiderers even use wool on cotton fabric. Danish Flower Thread is a thicker thread with a matte finish, one strand equaling two of cotton floss.

4. Embroidery hoop. Use a plastic or wooden 4″, 5″ or 6″ round or oval hoop with a screw type tension adjuster.

5. A pair of sharp embroidery scissors is absolutely essential.

Prepare the fabric by whipping, hemming or zigzagging on the sewing machine to prevent raveling at the edges. Next, locate the exact center of the design you have chosen, so that you can then center the design on the piece of fabric. Many of the designs in the book have an arrow at the top and along one side; follow the indicated rows to where they intersect; this is the center stitch. Next, find the center of the fabric by folding it in half both vertically and horizontally. The center stitch of the design should fall where the creases in the fabric meet.

It's usually not very convenient to begin work with the center stitch itself. As a rule it's better to start at the top of a design, working horizontal rows of a single color, left to right. This technique permits you to go from an unoccupied space to an occupied space (from an empty hole to a filled one), which makes ruffling the floss less likely. To find out where the top of the design should be placed, count squares up from the center of the design, and then count off the corresponding number of holes up from the center of the fabric.

Next, place the section of the fabric to be worked tautly in the hoop; the tighter the better, for tension makes it easier to push the needle through the holes without piercing the fabric. As you work, use the screw adjuster to tighten as necessary. Keep the screw at the top and out of your way.

Counted cross-stitch is very simple. When beginning, fasten thread with a waste knot by holding a bit of thread on the underside of the work and anchoring it with the first few stitches (*diagram 1*). To stitch, push the threaded needle up

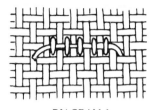

DIAGRAM 1
Reverse side of work

through a hole in the fabric and cross over the thread intersection (or square) diagonally, left to right (*diagram 2*). This

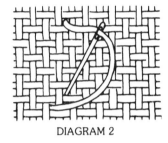

DIAGRAM 2

is half the stitch. Now cross back, right to left, making an X (*diagram 3*). Do all the stitches in the same color in the same

DIAGRAM 3

row, working left to right and slanting from bottom left to upper right (*diagram 3*). Then cross back, completing the X's (*diagram 4*). Some cross-stitchers prefer to cross each stitch

DIAGRAM 4

as they come to it; this is fine, but be sure the slant is always in the correct direction. Of course, isolated stitches must be crossed as you work them. Vertical stitches are crossed as shown in diagram 5. Holes are used more than once; all

DIAGRAM 5

stitches "hold hands" unless a space is indicated. The work is always held upright, never turned as for some needlepoint stitches.

When carrying a color from one area to another, wiggle your needle under existing stitches on the underside. Do not carry a color across an open expanse of fabric for more than a few stitches, as the thread will be visible from the front. Remember, in counted cross-stitch you do not work the background.

To end a color, weave in and out of the underside of stitches, perhaps making a scallop stitch or two for extra security (*diagram 6*). Whenever possible, end in the direction

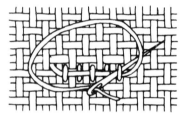

DIAGRAM 6
Reverse side of work

in which you are traveling, jumping up a row if necessary (*diagram 7*). This prevents holes caused by work being pulled in two directions. Do not make knots; knots make

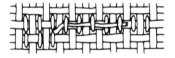

DIAGRAM 7
Reverse side of work

bumps. Cut off the ends of the threads; do not leave any tails because they'll show through when the work is mounted.

Another stitch used in counted cross-stitch is the back-

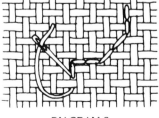

DIAGRAM 8

stitch. This is worked from hole to hole and may be vertical, horizontal or slanted (*diagram 8*). For a special effect, chain stitch may be recommended; this stitch can be worked in the normal fashion (*diagram 9*).

CHAIN STITCH

DIAGRAM 9

Working on linen requires a slightly different technique. Evenweave linen is remarkably regular, but there are always some thin threads and some that are nubbier or fatter than others. To even these out and to make a stitch that is easy to see, the cross-stitch is worked over two threads each way. The "square" you are covering is thus 4 threads (*diagram 10*). The first few stitches on linen are sometimes difficult, but one quickly begins "to see in twos." After the third stitch, a

DIAGRAM 10

pattern is established, and should you inadvertently cross over three threads instead of four, the difference in slant will make it immediately apparent that you have erred.

Linen evenweave fabric should be worked with the selvage at the side, not at the top and bottom.

Because you go over more threads, linen affords more variations in stitches. A half stitch can slant in either direction and is uncrossed. A three-fourths stitch is shown in diagram 11. Diagram 12 shows backstitch on linen.

Gingham or other checkered material can also be used for counted cross-stitch by making the crosses over the checks from corner to corner. If you wish to embroider a cross-stitch design onto a fabric that does not have an even weave, baste

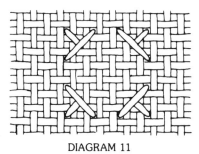

DIAGRAM 11

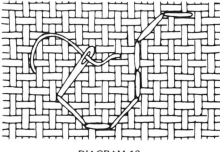

DIAGRAM 12

a lightweight Penelope canvas to the fabric. The design can then be worked from the chart by making crosses over the double mesh of the canvas, being careful not to catch the threads of the canvas in the sewing. When the design is completed, the basting stitches are removed, and the horizontal and then the vertical threads of the canvas are removed, one strand at a time, with a tweezers. The cross-stitch design will remain on the fabric.

After you have completed your embroidery, wash it in cool or lukewarm water with a mild soap. Rinse well. Do not wring. Roll in a towel to remove excess moisture. Immediately iron on a padded surface with the embroidery face down. Be sure the embroidery is completely dry before attempting to mount it.

To mount as a picture, center the embroidery over a pure white, rag-content mat board. Turn margins over to the back evenly. Lace the margins with sturdy thread, top to bottom, side to side. The fabric should be tight and even, with a little tension. Never use glue for mounting. Counted cross-stitch on cotton or linen may be framed under glass. Wool needs to breathe and should not be framed under glass unless a breathing space is left.

Charted designs can also be used for needlepoint. The designs can be worked directly onto needlepoint canvas by counting off the correct number of warp and weft squares shown on the chart, each square representing one stitch to be taken on the canvas. If you prefer to put some guidelines on the canvas, make certain that your marking medium is waterproof. Use either nonsoluble inks, acrylic paints thinned appropriately with water so as not to clog the holes in the canvas, or oil paints mixed with benzine or turpentine. Felt-tipped pens are very handy, but check the labels carefully because not all felt markers are waterproof. It is a good idea to experiment with any writing materials on a piece of scrap canvas to make certain that all material is waterproof. There is nothing worse than having a bit of ink run onto the needlepoint as you are blocking it.

There are two distinct types of needlepoint canvas: single-mesh and double-mesh. Double-mesh is woven with two horizontal and two vertical threads forming each mesh, whereas single-mesh is woven with one vertical and one horizontal thread forming each mesh. Double-mesh is a very stable canvas on which the threads will stay securely in place as you work. Single-mesh canvas, which is more widely used, is a little easier on the eyes because the spaces are slightly larger.

A tapestry needle with a rounded, blunt tip and an elongated eye is used for needlepoint. The most commonly used needle for #10 canvas is the #18 needle. The needle should clear the hole in the canvas without spreading the threads. Special yarns that have good twist and are sufficiently heavy to cover the canvas are used for needlepoint.

Although there are over a hundred different needlepoint

stitches, the *Tent Stitch* is universally considered to be *the* needlepoint stitch. The three most familiar versions of Tent Stitch are: Plain Half-Cross Stitch, Continental Stitch and Basket Weave Stitch.

Plain Half-Cross Stitch *(diagram 13)*. Always work Half-Cross Stitch from left to right, then turn the canvas around and work the return row, still stitching from left to right. Bring the needle to the front of the canvas at a point that will be the bottom of the first stitch. The needle is in a vertical position when making the stitch. Keep the stitches loose for minimum distortion and good coverage. This stitch must be worked on a double-mesh canvas.

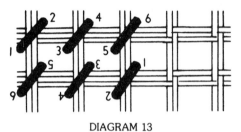

DIAGRAM 13

Continental Stitch *(diagram 14)*. Start this design at the upper right-hand corner and work from right to left. The needle is slanted and always brought out a mesh ahead. The resulting stitch is actually a Half-Cross Stitch on top and a slanting stitch on the back. When the row is finished, turn the canvas around and work the return row, still stitching from right to left.

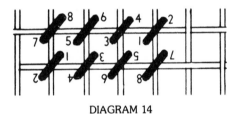

DIAGRAM 14

Basket Weave Stitch *(diagram 15)*. Start in the upper right-hand corner of the area with four Continental Stitches, two worked horizontally across the top and two placed directly below the first stitch. Then work diagonal rows, the first slanting up and across the canvas from right to left and the next down and across from left to right. Each new row is

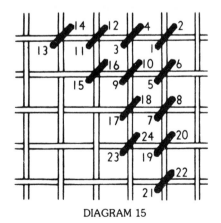

DIAGRAM 15

one stitch longer. As you go down the canvas (left to right), the needle is held in a vertical position; as you move in the opposite direction, the needle is horizonal. The rows should interlock, creating a basket-weave pattern on the reverse. If this is not done properly, a faint ridge will show where the pattern was interrupted. Always stop working in the middle of a row, rather than at the end, so that you will know in which direction you were working.

Bind all the raw edges of needlepoint canvas with masking tape, double-fold bias tape or even adhesive tape. There are no set rules on where to begin a design. Generally it is easier to begin close to the center and work outward toward the edges of the canvas, working the backgrounds or borders last. To avoid fraying the yarn, work with strands not longer than 18″.

When you have finished your needlepoint, it should be blocked. No matter how straight you have kept your work, blocking will give it a professional look.

Any hard, flat surface that you do not mind marring with nail holes and one that will not be warped by wet needlepoint can serve as a blocking board. A large piece of plywood, an old drawing board or an old-fashioned doily blocker are ideal.

Moisten a Turkish towel in cold water and roll the needlepoint in the towel. Leaving the needlepoint in the towel overnight will insure that both the canvas and the yarn are thoroughly and evenly dampened. Do not saturate the needlepoint! Never hold the needlepoint under the faucet as that much water is not necessary.

Mark the desired outline on the blocking board, making sure that the corners are straight. Lay the needlepoint on the blocking board, and tack the canvas with thumbtacks spaced about ½″ to ¾″ apart. It will probably take a good deal of pulling and tugging to get the needlepoint straight, but do not be afraid of this stress. Leave the canvas on the blocking board until thoroughly dry. Never put an iron on your needlepoint. You cannot successfully block with a steam iron because the needlepoint must dry in the straightened position. You may also have needlepoint blocked professionally. If you have a pillow made, a picture framed or a chair seat mounted, the craftsman may include the blocking in the price.

Charted designs can be worked in duplicate stitch over the squares formed by stockinette stitch in knitting or afghan stitch in crochet. The patterns can also be knitted directly into the work by working with more than one color, as in Fair Isle knitting. The wool not in use is always stranded across the back of the work. When it has to be stranded over more than five stitches, it should be twisted around the wool in use on every third stitch, thus preventing long strands at the back of the work. When several colors are used, a method known as "motif knitting" is employed. In this method short lengths of wool are cut and wound on bobbins, using a separate bobbin for each color and twisting the colors where they meet to avoid gaps in the work, as in knitting argyle socks.

Each of the designs has its own color key. The colors, however, are merely suggestions. You should feel free to substitute your own colors for the ones indicated, thereby creating a design that is uniquely yours. If you decide to create a new color scheme, work it out in detail before beginning a project. To give you a good idea of how the finished project will look, put tracing paper over the design in the book and experiment with your own colors on the tracing paper.

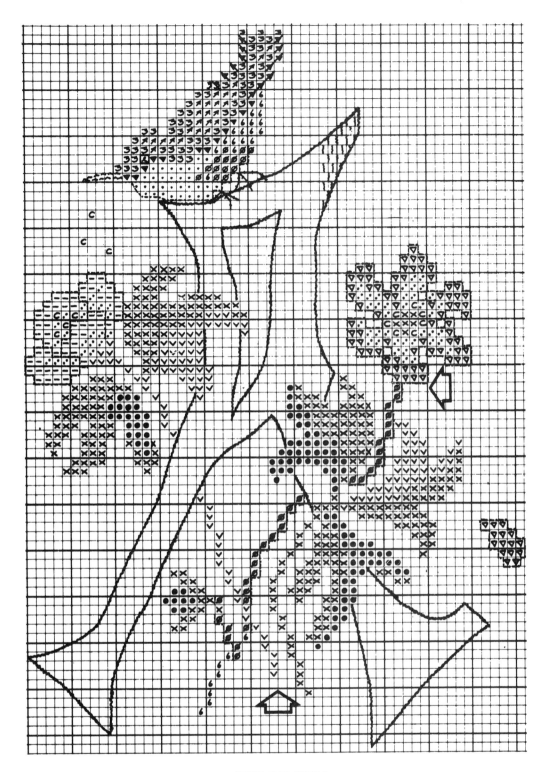

COLOR KEY

	DMC #			DMC #			DMC #	
⊟		snow white	C	726	light marigold	⅔	400	bright copper
⊡	819	ice pink	V	368	light moss green	↗	334	medium sky blue
▽	818	light pink	X	989	light grass green	③	312	dark sky blue
∅	224	light old rose	●	986	deep grass green	▼	336	medium navy
6	223	medium old rose	⊡	762	pale gray	⅄	310	black

Backstitch outline of letter (〰〰) with bright copper; fill interior of letter with counted cross-stitch or with backstitch (as shown). Backstitch flower, stem and bird outlines (—•—•—) with light pink. Backstitch bird's eye and tail feathers (———) with white and bird's feet (+++) with medium marigold (725).

7

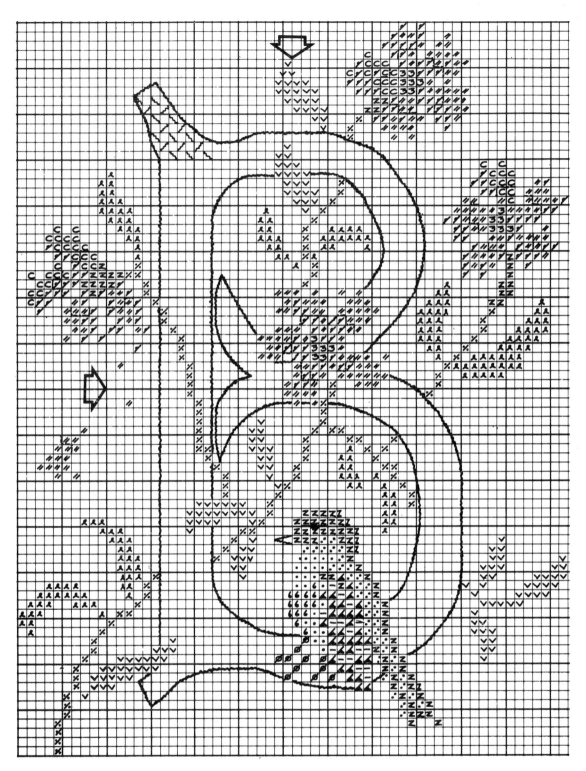

COLOR KEY

	DMC #			DMC #			DMC #	
─		snow white	6	307	medium yellow	1	905	bright emerald green
C	3326	dark pink	Ø	742	light yellow-orange	·	3013	light khaki green
/	899	light carnation pink	3	729	medium mustard	Z	3012	medium khaki green
Z	335	medium carnation pink	%	704	pale kelly green	▲	3011	dark khaki green
·	445	light yellow	V	906	medium emerald green	3	400	bright copper

Backstitch outline of letter and bird's beak ($\sim\sim$) with bright copper; fill interior of letter with counted cross-stitch or with backstitch, forming a "T" design (as shown). Backstitch bird's eye (———) with black (310). Backstitch flower petals (—·—·—) with dark carnation pink (326).

8

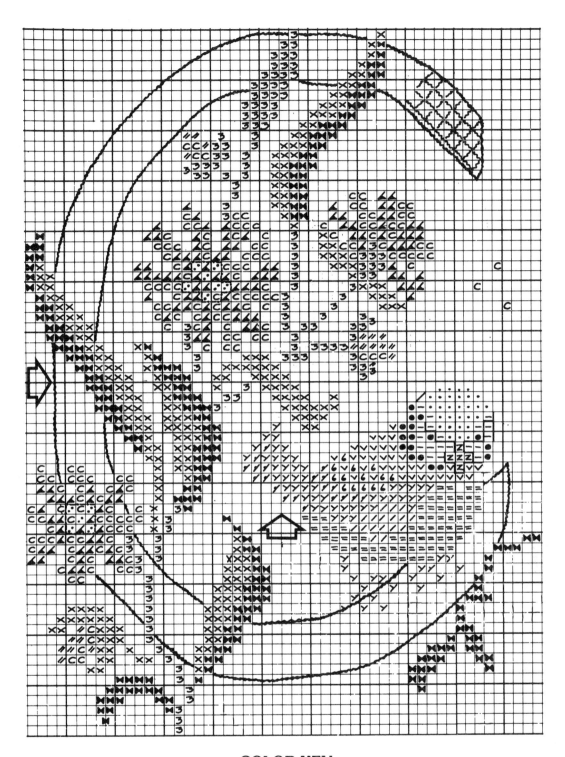

COLOR KEY

	DMC #	
⊟		snow white
⧄	307	medium yellow
⊟	444	dark yellow
⧄	553	medium lilac
C	996	light electric blue
◢	995	bright electric blue

	DMC #	
⊡	932	light soldier blue
⊠	931	medium soldier blue
⧄	930	dark soldier blue
X	989	light grass green
3	3347	medium spring green
⋈	905	bright emerald green

	DMC #	
V	3052	medium sage
6	3051	dark sage
⌐	400	bright copper
⊡	415	silver gray
Z	317	dark gray
●	310	black

Backstitch outline of letter (ᴧᴧᴧᴧ) with bright copper; fill interior of letter with counted cross-stitch or with backstitch, forming a diamond pattern (as shown). Backstitch around flower center (—·—·—) with silver gray. Backstitch bird's face (———) with black.

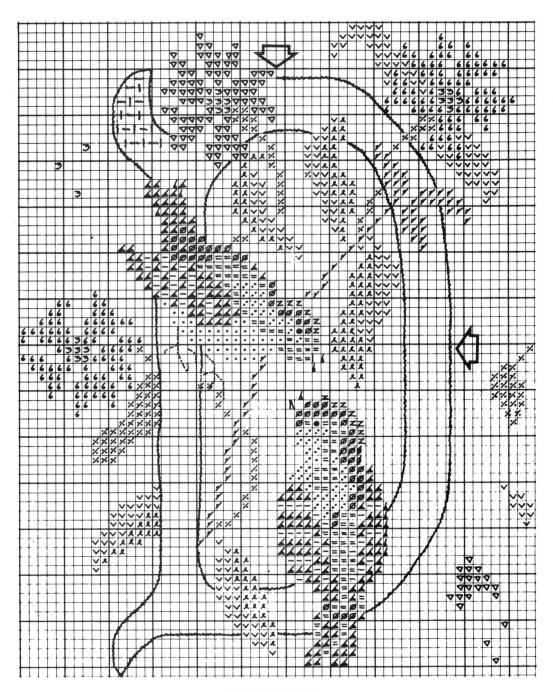

COLOR KEY

	DMC #			DMC #			DMC #	
⊟		snow white	⊿	581	light apple green	⊡	842	light brown
⊠	760	medium rose	⊽	906	medium emerald green	⊜	841	dusty brown
▽	3328	bright rose	⅄	905	bright emerald green	∅	840	medium brown
⬤	347	dark rose	⋅	644	medium ash	▲	839	dark brown
3	729	medium mustard	⌣	400	bright copper	⬤	310	black
▨	3348	light spring green						

Backstitch outline of letter (〰〰) with bright copper; fill interior of letter with counted cross-stitch or with backstitch, forming a geometric pattern (as shown). Backstitch bird's beak (———) with dark brown and bird's feet (—·—·—) with medium mustard.

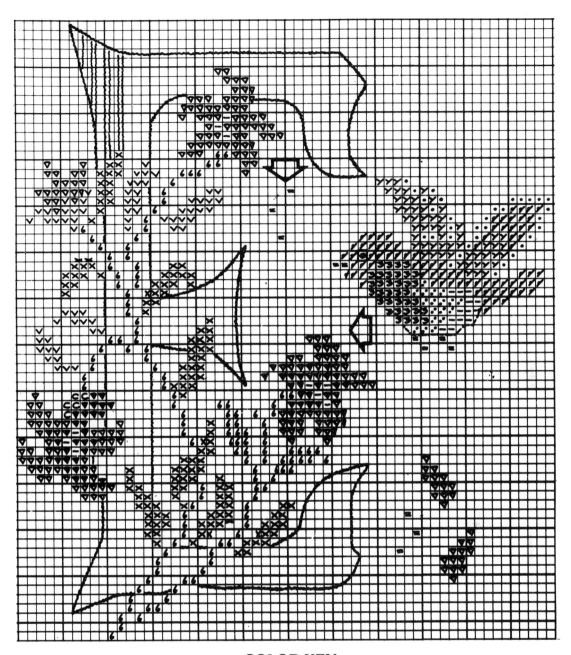

COLOR KEY

	DMC #			DMC #			DMC #	
⊟	822	ash	▽	553	medium lilac	☑	907	light emerald green
⊡	352	medium peach	▼	552	bright lilac	☒	906	medium emerald green
③	351	bright peach	⊡	932	light soldier blue	☑	905	bright emerald green
⊟	725	medium marigold	☑	931	medium soldier blue	☒	400	bright copper
⊂	554	light lilac	☑	930	dark soldier blue	⬤	310	black

Backstitch outline of letter (〰〰) with bright copper; fill interior of letter with counted cross-stitch or with chain stitch (as shown). Backstitch bird (—·—·—) with bright pink.

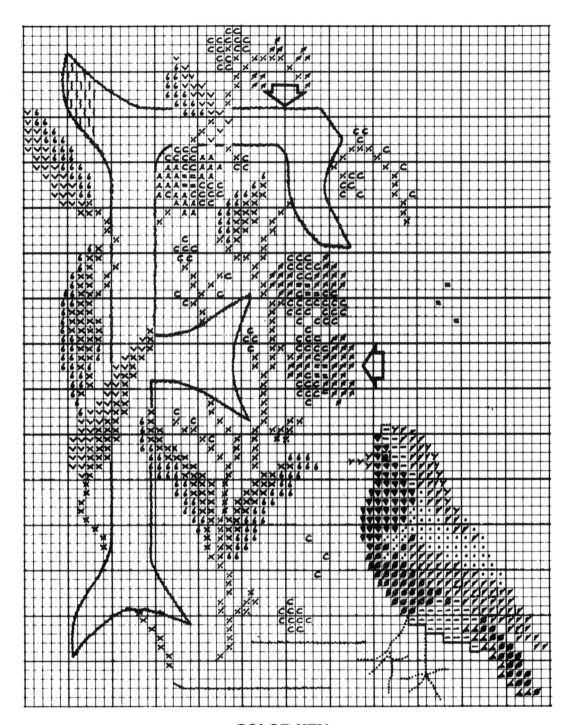

COLOR KEY

DMC #			DMC #			DMC #		
⊡	761	light rose	⊼	798	dark Dresden blue	⌇	905	bright emerald green
⊘	3328	bright rose	·	932	light soldier blue	⊠	3347	medium spring green
▲	919	medium sienna	⊻	931	medium soldier blue	⊠	400	bright copper
−	725	medium marigold	⊿	930	dark soldier blue	⊟	762	pale gray
⊅	809	medium Dresden blue	⋁	907	light emerald green	▼	413	deep gray
c	799	bright Dresden blue	⊠	906	medium emerald green	●	310	black

Backstitch outline of letter and ground lines (ᴧᴧᴧᴧ) with bright copper; fill interior of letter with counted cross-stitch or with backstitch (as shown). Backstitch bird's eye and wing (·—·—·) with pale gray, bird's head and feet (··· ···) with medium soldier blue and bird's belly (———) with bright rose.

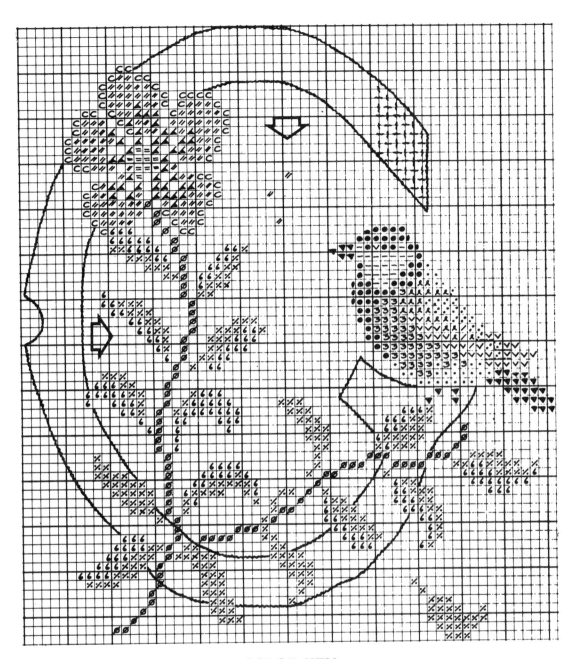

COLOR KEY

	DMC #	
⊟		snow white
⊟	725	medium marigold
·	307	medium yellow
3	444	dark yellow
C	3326	dark pink
⊘	335	medium carnation pink

	DMC #	
◢	309	bright carnation pink
∨	926	medium teal
▼	924	dark teal
⊘	3012	medium khaki green
⊠	3347	medium spring green
◖	3346	dark spring green

	DMC #	
⊡	3052	medium sage
⊼	3051	dark sage
⊘	762	pale gray
⋈	400	bright copper
◉	310	black

Backstitch outline of letter (〰〰) with bright copper; fill interior of letter with counted cross-stitch or with backstitch, forming a close geometric pattern (as shown). Backstitch bird's wing (·—·—·) with pale gray.

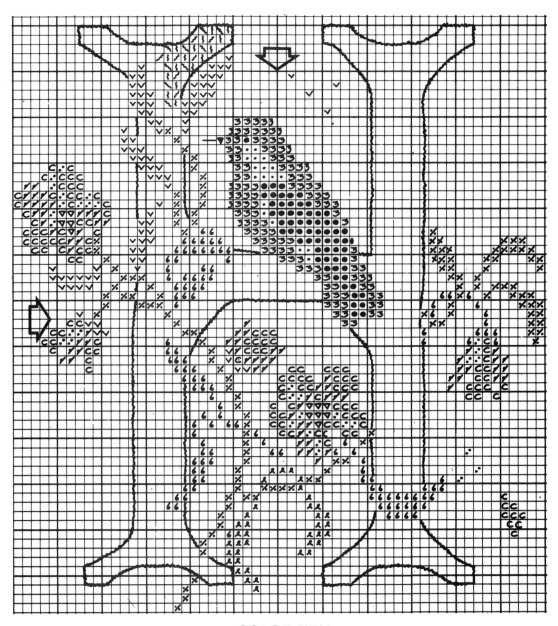

COLOR KEY

	DMC #			DMC #			DMC #	
▽	726	light marigold	☑	826	bright blue	◪	702	medium kelly green
·	307	medium yellow	Ⅵ	906	medium emerald green	▼	976	medium raisin
3	444	dark yellow	𝘅	905	bright emerald green	♫	400	bright copper
·	210	medium lavender	☒	703	light kelly green	●	310	black
C	813	medium blue						

Backstitch outline of letter (〰〰) with bright copper; fill interior of letter with counted cross-stitch or with backstitch (as shown). Backstitch birds' face (—·—·—) with black and bird's beak (———) with medium raisin.

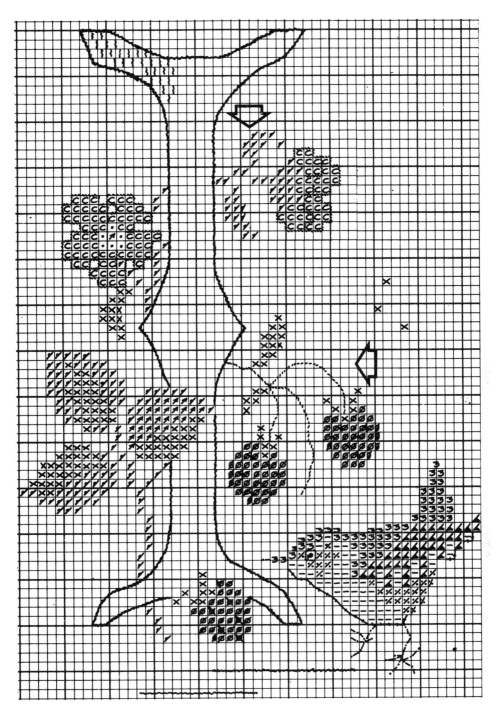

COLOR KEY

DMC #		
C		snow white
Ø	350	dark peach
·	725	medium marigold
⊠	907	light emerald green
↗	368	light moss green

DMC #		
X	989	light grass green
⊿	988	medium grass green
⊟	3033	light sand
⊿	612	light olive brown

DMC #		
3	611	medium olive brown
◣	610	dark olive brown
⟮	400	bright copper
●	310	black

Backstitch outline of letter and ground lines (〰〰〰) with bright copper; fill interior of letter with counted cross-stitch or with backstitch (as shown). Backstitch bird's tail and breast (–⫻–⫻–) with dark olive brown, bird's feet (–·—·–) with medium olive brown and bird's eye (· · · · ·) with black. Backstitch branches and flower petals (· · · · · · ·) with light emerald green.

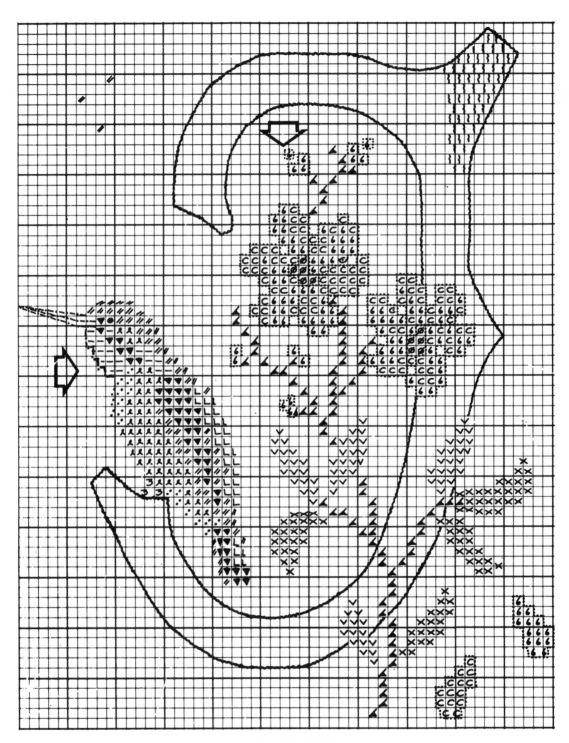

COLOR KEY

DMC #			DMC #			DMC #		
⊡	760	medium rose	⊠	831	light bronze	⊠	988	medium grass green
⊥	3328	bright rose	⊔	519	medium cornflower	◢	987	deep grass green
⊟	677	pale mustard	⊘	518	bright cornflower	⅔	400	bright copper
C	307	medium yellow	▼	517	dark cornflower	³	414	medium gray
6	444	dark yellow	⊽	989	light grass green	◉	310	black

Backstitch outline of letter (ᴧᴧᴧᴧ) with bright copper; fill interior of letter with counted cross-stitch or with backstitch (as shown). Backstitch bird's beak and neck (—·—·—) with medium gray. Backstitch flowers and petals (······) with light grass green.

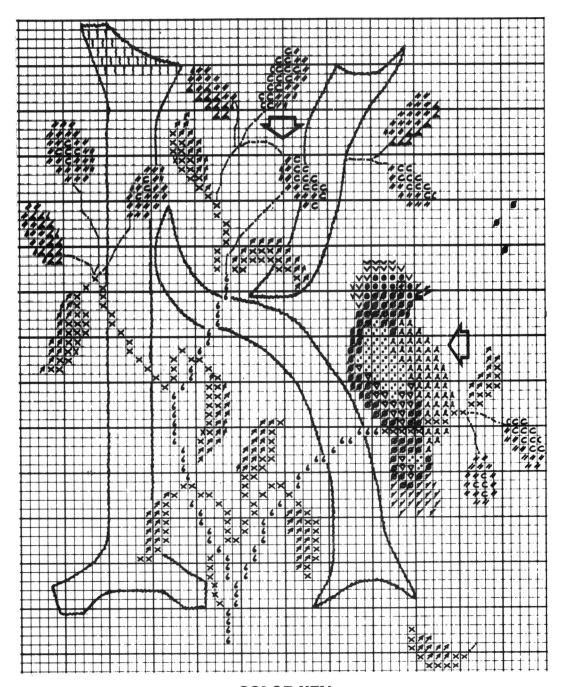

COLOR KEY

	DMC #	
C	3688	light dusty rose
◿	3687	medium dusty rose
◣	3685	dark dusty rose
↗	3348	light spring green
✕	3347	medium spring green

	DMC #	
◢	3345	hunter green
▽	415	silver gray
⊡	738	ice tan
▽	437	light tan
⊘	436	medium tan

	DMC #	
Ⅺ	434	dark tan
⅀	400	bright copper
⊅	433	light chocolate brown
◐	898	dark chocolate brown

Backstitch outline of letter (〰〰) with bright copper; fill interior of letter with counted cross-stitch or with backstitch (as shown). Backstitch bird's feet and lower portion of beak (———) with dark chocolate brown, and bird's eyes (·····) with silver gray. Backstitch branches (—·—·—) with medium spring green.

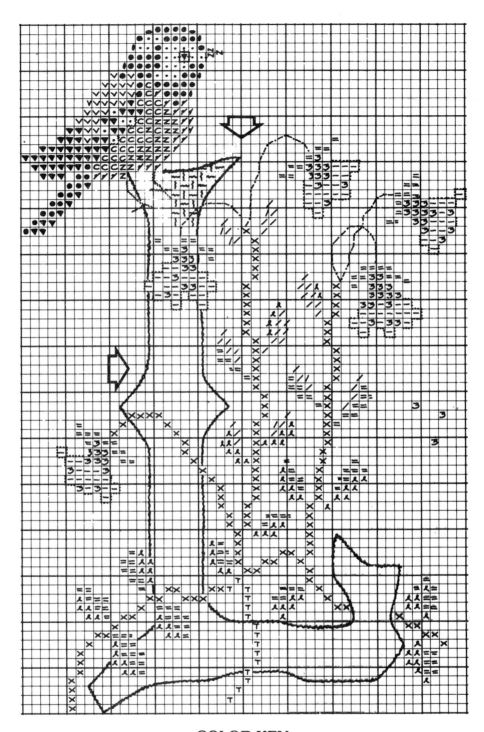

COLOR KEY

DMC #			DMC #			DMC #	
·		snow white	−	3078	sunshine yellow	⊿	907	light emerald green
c	3033	light sand	V	926	medium teal	=	906	medium emerald green
z	3024	pale gunmetal	▼	924	dark teal	𝍤	905	bright emerald green
⟋	3023	light gunmetal	T	3052	medium sage green	𝈀	400	bright copper
N	433	light chocolate brown	X	3012	medium khaki green	◉	310	black
3	351	bright peach						

Backstitch outline of letter (ᨆᨆᨆ) with bright copper; fill interior of letter with counted cross-stitch or with backstitch, forming a close geometric pattern (as shown). Backstitch bird's eye (+−+−+) with black and bird's feet (ıııııı) with medium teal. Backstitch flowers (· · · · ·) with bright peach and branches (−·−·−) with medium khaki green.

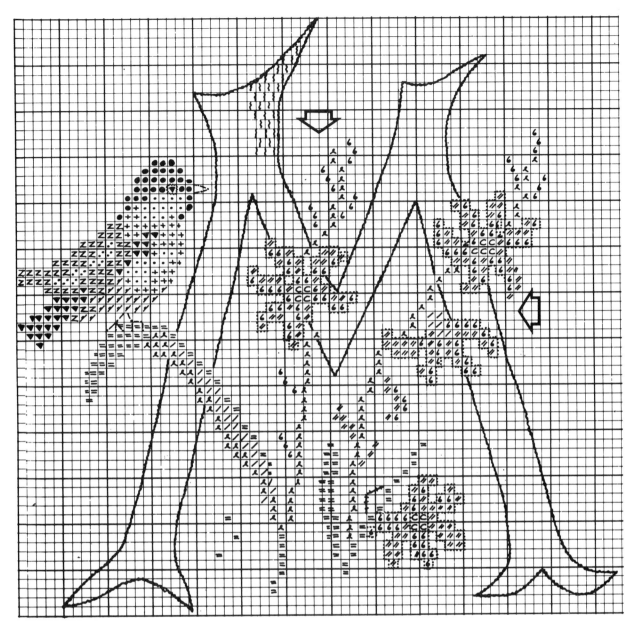

COLOR KEY

	DMC #	
C	743	dark lemon yellow
⊘	742	light yellow-orange
⚡	740	dark yellow-orange
·	644	medium ash
z	642	coconut brown

	DMC #	
▼	640	dark coconut brown
·	762	pale gray
+	415	silver gray
⟋	318	light gray
⟋	907	light emerald green

	DMC #	
=	906	medium emerald green
人	905	bright emerald green
⚡	400	bright copper
●	311	light navy

Backstitch outline of letter (⋀⋀⋀) with bright copper; fill interior of letter with counted cross-stitch or with backstitch (as shown). Backstitch bird's eye (⁛⁛⁛⁛) with pale gray and bird's beak and legs (—·—·—) with dark coconut brown. Backstitch petals (••••••) with light pumpkin (947) and branches (┼┼┼) with light emerald green.

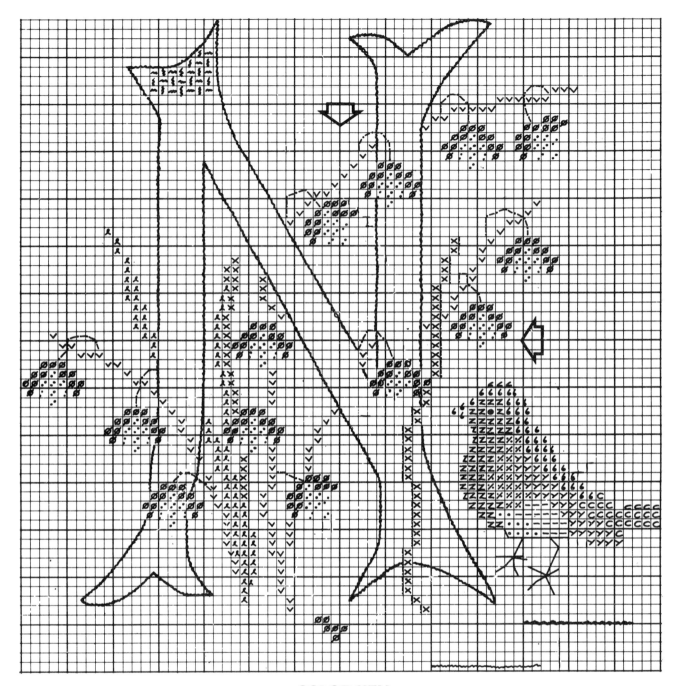

COLOR KEY

DMC #		DMC #		DMC #	
·	snow white	··	955 iced baby green	c	841 dusty brown
−	822 ash	V	704 pale kelly green	⊠	840 medium brown
Z	3328 bright rose	X	703 light kelly green	6	839 dark brown
Ø	356 medium salmon	⅄	905 bright emerald green	●	310 black
⊠	794 light copen blue	⸗	400 bright copper		

Backstitch outline of letter and ground lines (∿∿∿) with bright copper; fill interior of letter with counted cross-stitch or with backstitch, forming a close geometric pattern (as shown). Backstitch bird's feet (———) with dark brown. Backstitch stems (—·—·—) with bright emerald green.

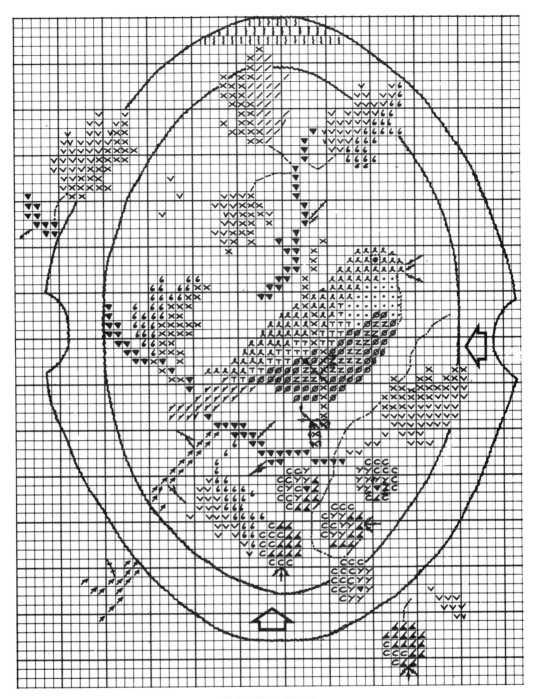

COLOR KEY

	DMC #	
C	743	dark lemon yellow
⊠	947	light pumpkin
⊡	368	light moss green
⊽	989	light grass green
⊠	988	medium grass green
⚅	987	dark grass green

	DMC #	
·	739	ice brown
T	437	light tan
⊿	436	medium tan
⊘	435	bright tan
⊿	434	dark tan

	DMC #	
人	433	light chocolate brown
↗	841	dusty brown
▼	839	dark brown
⅃	400	bright copper
●	310	black

Backstitch outline of letter (∧∧∧) with bright copper; fill interior of letter with counted cross-stitch or with backstitch (as shown). Backstitch branches and bird's beak and legs (‐╫‐╫‐) with dark brown. Backstitch bird's breast (∖∖∖∖∖) with medium tan. Backstitch stems and vine (‐·‐·‐) with dark grass green. Backstitch branches (╅╅╅) with dusty brown.

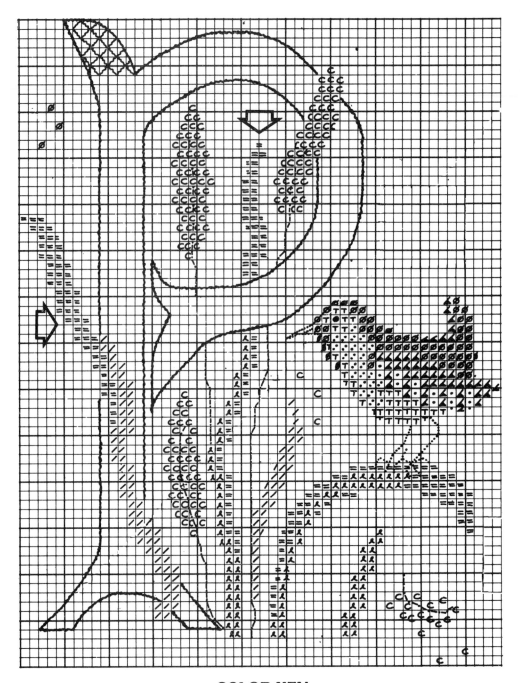

COLOR KEY

	DMC #			DMC #			DMC #	
•		snow white	⚹	905	bright emerald green	⌐	400	bright copper
C	996	light electric blue	⊡	3047	light khaki brown	◢	869	dark acorn
⊘	907	light emerald green	T	3046	medium khaki brown	●	433	light chocolate brown
⚌	906	medium emerald green	Ø	3045	dark khaki brown			

Backstitch outline of letter (∿∿∿) with bright copper; fill interior of letter with counted cross-stitch or with backstitch, forming a diamond pattern (as shown). Backstitch bird's beak and legs (· · · · ·) with dark acorn. Backstitch stems (—·—·—) with medium emerald green.

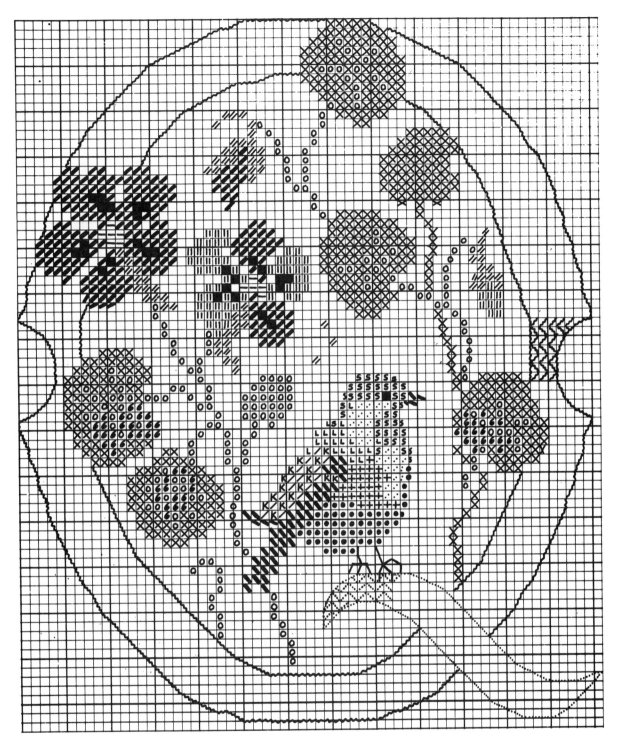

COLOR KEY

	DMC #			DMC #			DMC #	
⊡		ecru	◎	907	light emerald green	⊘	3046	medium khaki brown
＋	3689	pale dusty rose	✕	906	medium emerald green	∟	841	dusty brown
◣	3354	light dusty pink	◢	905	bright emerald green	S	839	dark brown
⊟	973	canary yellow	⊘	3024	pale gunmetal	∴	435	bright tan
Ⅲ	947	light pumpkin	K	3023	light gunmetal	♪	433	light chocolate brown
⊿	900	dark pumpkin	N	3022	medium gunmetal	■	938	deep chocolate brown

Backstitch outline of letter with light chocolate brown (ᴧᴧᴧᴧ) and with bright tan (·····); fill interior portions of letter in matching color with counted cross-stitch or with backstitch, forming a herringbone pattern (as shown). Backstitch bird's feet and beak (———) with medium gunmetal.

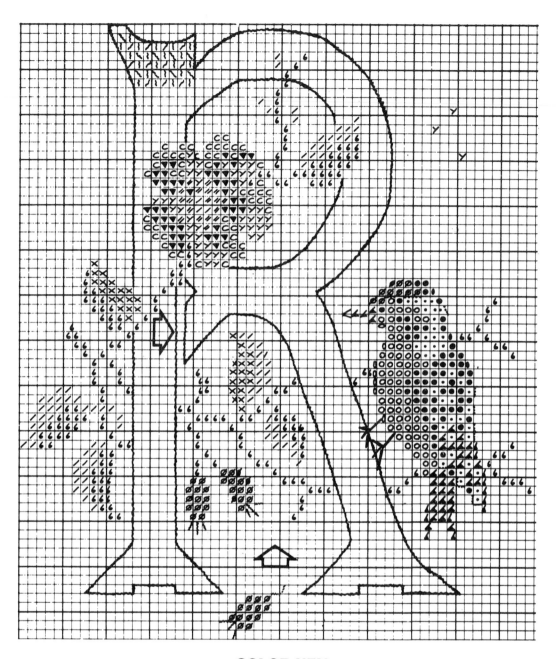

COLOR KEY

DMC #		
·	snow white	
⊻	899	light carnation pink
▼	335	medium carnation pink
C	776	medium pink
⊘	3328	bright rose

DMC #		
⊘	725	medium marigold
⁄	368	light moss green
☒	989	light grass green
6	988	medium grass green

DMC #		
▲	500	dark lichen
◐	422	beige
⅁	400	bright copper
◉	310	black

Backstitch outline of letter and bud tips (⌒⌒⌒) with bright copper; fill interior of letter with counted cross-stitch or with backstitch (as shown). Backstitch bird (·······) with black, bird's beak (<) with dark lichen and bird's feet (———) with medium gray (414). Backstitch bud stem (⁗⁗⁗⁗) with medium grass green.

COLOR KEY

DMC #			DMC #			DMC #	
⊡	712	ivory	⬢	3346	dark spring green	⟦	400	bright copper
⊟	950	oatmeal	⊡	3024	pale gunmetal	▽	841	dusty brown
⊂	603	dark hot pink	③	3023	light gunmetal	⟦	839	dark brown
◣	602	light magenta	⬀	3022	medium gunmetal	◉	310	black
☑	3347	medium spring green					

Backstitch outline of letter (⌁⌁⌁) with bright copper; fill interior of letter with counted cross-stitch or with backstitch (as shown). Backstitch bird's eye (—•—•—) with ivory, bird's feet (———) with medium gunmetal and bird's breast (ıııııı) with dark brown. Backstitch stems (—·—·—) with dark spring green and flowers (·····) with medium yellow (307).

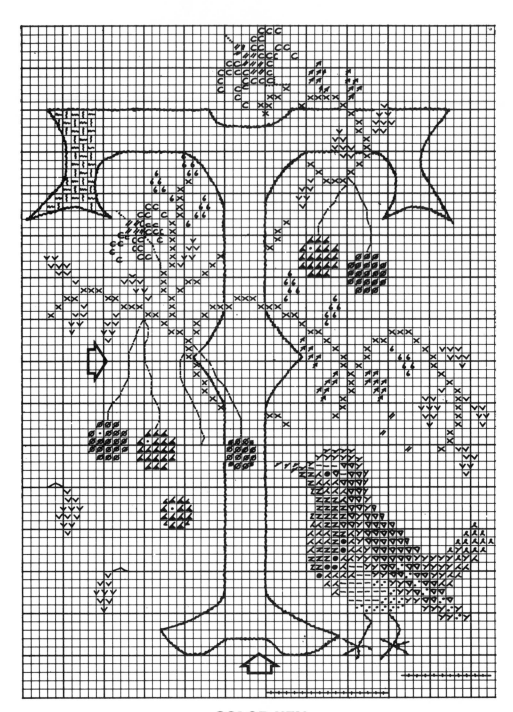

COLOR KEY

	DMC #			DMC #			DMC #	
⊟	712	ivory	©	3326	dark pink	⊿	414	medium gray
∵	644	medium ash	⊠	799	bright Dresden blue	⅌	400	bright copper
⊠	436	medium tan	⊻	989	light grass green	▽	841	dusty brown
⊡	754	medium flesh	⊠	988	medium grass green	⊠	840	medium brown
▲	817	cherry	⑥	987	dark grass green	Ⅰ	839	dark brown
∅	347	dark rose	↗	3347	medium spring green	●	310	black
⧄	335	medium carnation pink						

Backstitch outline of letter (∿∿∿) with bright copper; fill interior of letter with counted cross-stitch or with backstitch, forming a close geometric pattern (as shown). Backstitch bird's legs (–●–●–) with medium gray. Backstitch ground lines (–+–+–) with medium brown. Backstitch cherry stems (–·–·–) with medium spring green and leaf stems (———) with light grass green. Backstitch flowers (·····) with medium carnation pink.

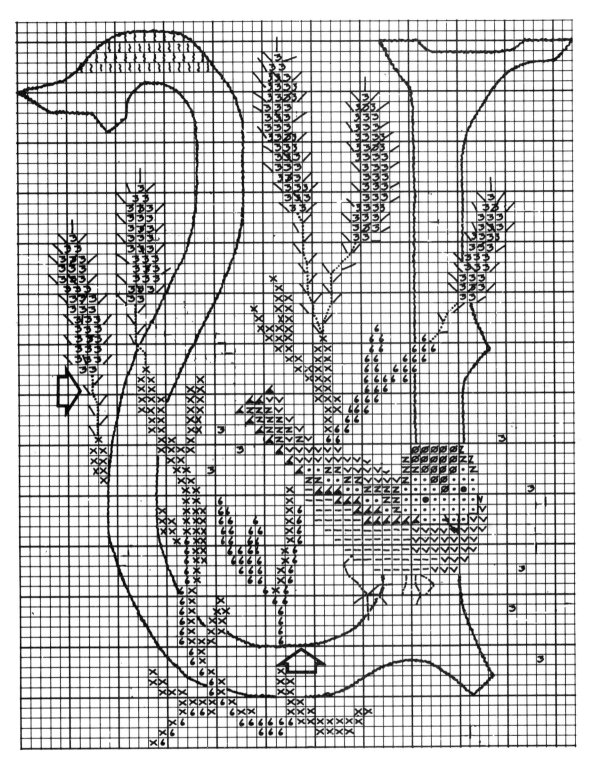

COLOR KEY

	DMC #	
⊠	3328	bright rose
③	444	dark yellow
⊠	906	medium emerald green
◪	905	bright emerald green

	DMC #	
⊡	3033	light sand
⊟	842	light brown
▽	841	dusty brown
⊿	840	medium brown

	DMC #	
◢	839	dark brown
◿	400	bright copper
◉	310	black

Backstitch outline of letter (〜〜〜) with bright copper; fill interior of letter with counted cross-stitch or with backstitch (as shown). Backstitch bird's beak (—•—•—) with black and bird's feet (—•—•—) with medium gray (414). Backstitch stems (•••••) with dark yellow and lines on flowers (———) with medium brown.

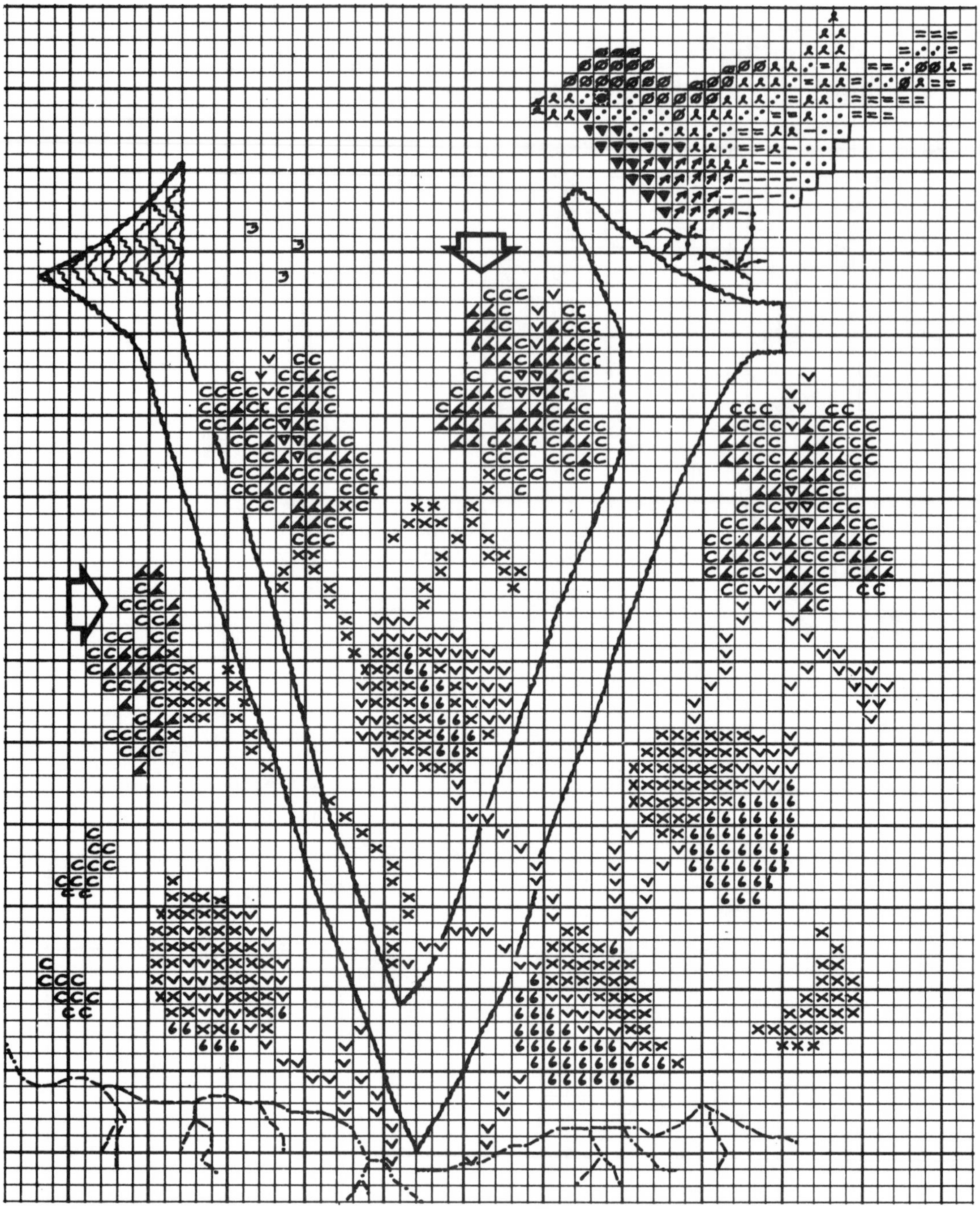

COLOR KEY

	DMC #			DMC #			DMC #	
•	712	ivory	3	680	dark mustard	⁚	644	medium ash
–	352	medium peach	C	553	medium lilac	=	642	coconut brown
↗	351	bright peach	◢	552	bright lilac	⅄	640	dark coconut brown
Ø	350	dark peach	V	907	light emerald green	⊔	400	bright copper
▼	349	red-orange	☒	906	medium emerald green	●	310	black
▽	725	medium marigold	6	905	bright emerald green			

Backstitch outline of letter (⋀⋀⋀) with bright copper; fill interior of letter with counted cross-stitch or with backstitch, forming a herringbone pattern (as shown). Backstitch bird's eye (•••••••) with ivory, bird's feet (—•—•—•—) with dark coconut brown and bird's body (———) with red-orange. Backstitch roots (–•—•—) with dark mustard.

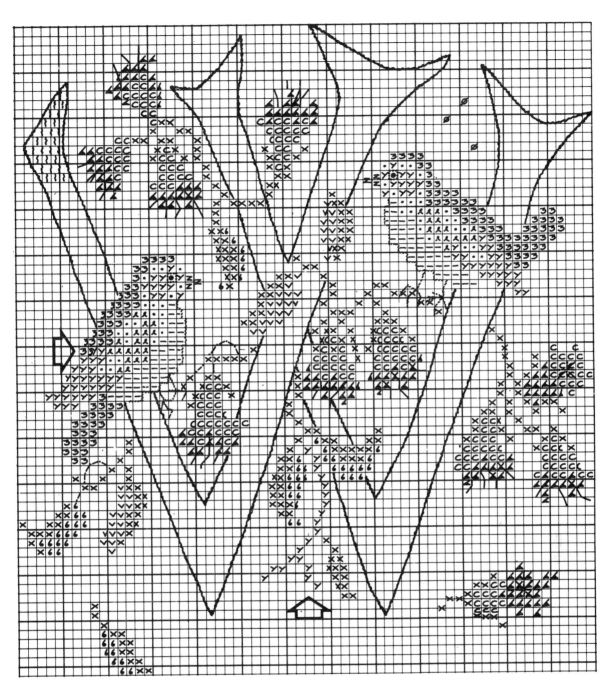

COLOR KEY

DMC #			DMC #			DMC #		
⊡		snow white	☑	907	light emerald green	⊠	400	bright copper
⊟	950	oatmeal	⊠	906	medium emerald green	☑	840	medium brown
⊡	603	dark hot pink	⚅	905	bright emerald green	⚄	839	dark brown
◣	601	medium magenta	③	3045	dark khaki brown	⬤	310	black
⊘	444	dark yellow						

Backstitch outline of letter (⋀⋀⋀⋀) with bright copper; fill interior of letter with counted cross-stitch or with backstitch (as shown). Backstitch birds' eyes (• • • • •) with white and birds' breasts and feet (⟋ ⟋ ⟋ ⟋ ⟋) with medium brown. Backstitch flower stamens (———) with dark yellow and stems (—•—•—) with medium emerald green.

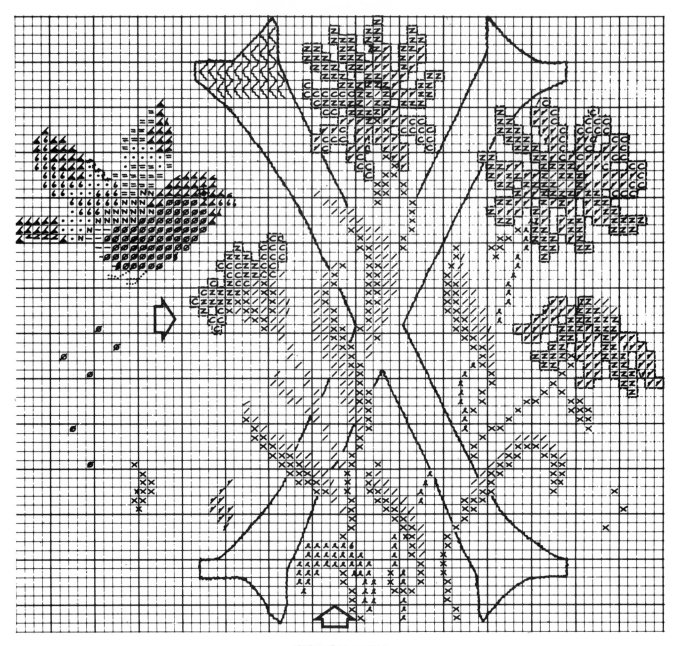

COLOR KEY

DMC #			DMC #			DMC #		
·		snow white	⊘	352	medium peach	6	640	dark coconut brown
C	445	light yellow	∕	3348	light spring green	⅃	400	bright copper
Z	307	medium yellow	⊠	3347	medium spring green	⩘	336	medium navy
⊘	444	dark yellow	⅃	3346	dark spring green	N	318	light gray
−	754	medium flesh	=	642	coconut brown	●	310	black

Backstitch outline of letter (∧∧∧∧) with bright copper; fill interior of letter with counted cross-stitch or with backstitch, forming a herringbone pattern (as shown). Backstitch bird's eye (-+-+-) with white, bird's feet (·····) with dark coconut brown and bird's wing (-+-+-) with black. Backstitch flower petals (—·—·—) with dark yellow and flower centers (———) with medium green.

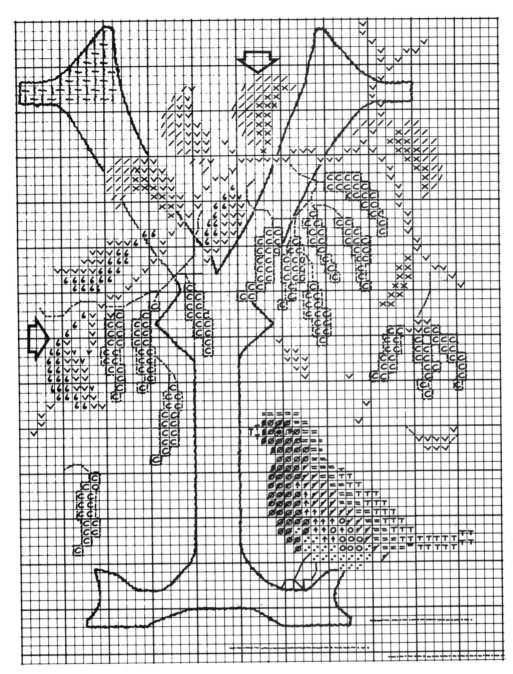

COLOR KEY

DMC #			DMC #			DMC #		
C	3078	snow white and sunshine yellow	↑	794	light copen blue	⊤	841	dusty brown
·	762	pale gray	⊘	368	light moss green	⊟	840	medium brown
○	644	medium ash	V	989	light grass green	⊘	839	dark brown
⊘	3328	bright rose	⊠	988	medium grass green	⅌	400	bright copper
			6	987	dark grass green	●	310	black

Backstitch outline of letter (⋀⋀⋀⋀) with bright copper; fill interior of letter with counted cross-stitch or with backstitch, forming a close geometric pattern (as shown). Backstitch bird's eye (· · · · ·) with a combination of sunshine yellow and snow white and bird's feet (———) with medium brown. Backstitch ground lines and stems (–·–·–) with light grass green.

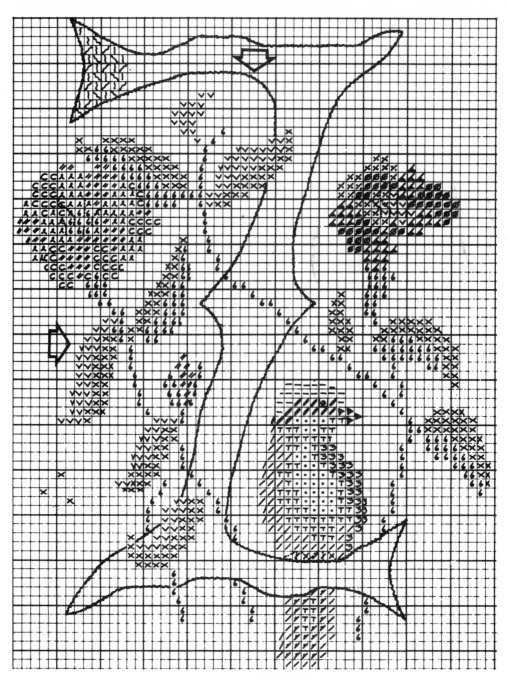

COLOR KEY

DMC #		DMC #		DMC #	
C 3326	bright rose	X 906	medium emerald green	801	medium chocolate brown
335	medium carnation pink	905	bright emerald green	L 400	bright copper
309	bright carnation pink	T 738	iced tan	318	light gray
606	dark orange-red	· 739	iced brown	317	dark gray
Ø 321	light ruby	437	light tan	310	black
815	burgundy	3 434	dark tan		
V 907	light emerald green	436	medium tan		

Backstitch outline of letter with bright copper; fill interior of letter with counted cross-stitch or with backstitch, forming a geometric pattern (as shown). Backstitch bird's eye (———) with iced brown and bird's feet (— · — · —) with dark gray. Backstitch flower centers (· · · · ·) with dark yellow (444).